Take Your

Shoes

Off First

Praise for

Take Your Shoes Off First

"*Take Your Shoes Off First* is an easy and entertaining read, that inspires deep reflection and a desire to engage from a more open and empathetic place. When people 'take their shoes off first' they lay the groundwork for better conversations and deeper connections – exactly what we all need to thrive in our diverse and changing world."

- *Bev Kaye, Wall Street Journal Bestselling Author of "Love'em or Lose'em"*

"I wish I had read this book many years ago. There are several critical times in my life I would have handled differently if I had. I will be thinking of the lessons in here often going forward both as a partner and a leader. I agree, the world would be a better place if more people worked to 'take their shoes off first.'"

- *Greg Amrofell, Chief Marketing Officer, IHME*

"Wow! This book was eye-opening and thought provoking! It held my attention throughout, and I want to read it again. It feels like it is one of those books I will keep re-reading. I want to implement the concepts in this book into every aspect of my human interactions - with my friends, family, partner, children, colleagues, even the stranger at the grocery store. I loved how you can see yourself in the book no matter the role you play. I would recommend this book for anyone and everyone!"

- *April Com, Military Wife and Stay at Home Mom*

"This book is made for the times we live in – short, entertaining, and thought provoking, with a focus on embracing change and being more inclusive. What could be better? Read it and then share it. You won't regret it."

- *Simon Shackleton, Senior VP of Sales and Marketing, Hartzell Aerospace*

"A unique and universal truth - that is what this book delivers in a concise entertaining package! Simple delivery of a powerful idea that is reminiscent of 'The Magic of Tidying Up' and 'The Happiness Project' in the eye-opening 'of course!' kind of way. It is relevant to everyone and easy to read. It's the perfect 'Today Show' segment!"

- *Amy Neuberger, MBA, serial entrepreneur*

"I loved it!! So much good stuff that got my wheels spinning for how I can apply this idea myself and with clients - What is possible in the world when I start with 'taking off my shoes first'?"

-    *Kathy Clayton, Executive Coach*

"Feeling stuck? Need your people to be more receptive to your ideas or change? Read this book. It is a quick read with lots of good ideas to help you improve your approach AND your results."

-    *John Hinds, MBA, Org Design, Development and Change Management Director, Banfield*

"Thank you for writing this powerful book! It is beautifully written and an amazing read! I so appreciated the combination of an absorbing story and easily implemented take away lessons! I used it immediately to help my husband through a sticky work situation. After discussing the book and some thoughtful consideration, he decided to rethink his approach. The next day he reported "I'm going to be taking my shoes off first more often! That made a big difference!"

-    *Lori Tanner, Chief Marketing and Business Development Officer, Accel 180*

"Reading this book made me feel like something cracked open. It inspired me to think more holistically and calmly about what is going right, where I'm stuck, what I want to do differently, and what I'm frustrated with about others and in myself. I was highlighting like crazy! It's engaging without being too cute, wise without being preachy, and motivational without being annoying. I want to use this on all our client engagements as a means for setting the stage for change work."

- *Jill Sherensky, CEO, Denny Mountain and Aquarian Consultants*

"This quick enlightening story reminds me of The Alchemist, The Celestine Prophecy, and A Course of Miracles - but with a business twist. I eagerly tagged along with Steve on his hero's journey to reawaken, evolve, and reconnect with people and the world around him. I wish I had this smart book when I was in the US Army. This is an essential guide for business professionals and organizational leaders about a powerful idea we should all take to heart."

- *Nancy Adams Treder, Public Relations Consultant*

Take Your Shoes Off First

A story about a simple idea with the power

to change everything for the better.

JULIA FREELAND

ORDERING INFORMATION

Quantity Sales: Special discounts are available on quantity purchases by corporations, associations, and others. For details, email info@revolveyou.com.

Individual Sales: *Take Your Shoes Off First* can be ordered directly from revolveyou.com and is available for purchase from all major bookstores and online book sellers.

Orders for college textbook / course adoption use. Please reach out at info@revolveyou.com for bulk discounts and curriculum options.

DISCUSSION GUIDES AND COURSES

Additional discussion guides, workshop outlines and micro-lessons are available at revolveyou.com. For facilitation help, speaking engagements and in person workshops, contact info@revolveyou.com.

Library of Congress catalogued as

ISBN 978-1-7374390-0-4

For all who stood by me as I struggled to find my way to better - thank you for caring enough to help me open to possibilities so I could see the world more clearly.

Contents

Why Read This Book?

If there was one thing I could do to make the world a better place and improve the quality of life of every individual, it would be to teach people how to 'take their shoes off first.'

This oft forgotten step in our life journeys is a powerful catalyst for achieving breakthroughs in both work and life. I have felt the magic of this simple idea transform me in some of the darkest days of my life. I have also seen it send shock waves through an organization and shine brilliant light on the lives of my clients many times over.

The short story within this book illustrates a fundamental concept that is critical to achieving breakthroughs and overcoming adversity. If you

1

are facing a big change, feeling stuck, longing for deeper, more fulfilling relationships with less conflict and more collaboration, or if you are just ready for your next breakthrough, this book was made for you.

If this book was given to you, consider yourself cared for. After you read it, you may feel like sharing it with someone you care for too.

How could one simple idea change everything? Give me one hour of your time and I will show you.

Your path to better is near. If you are willing to do the work, you will find it.

My Shoes

While seeking to return to my career as a Director of Learning and People Development, I found nothing but closed doors and narrow mindedness. I had been out of my career for 10 years raising my kids and the long-held vision of a stay-at-home mom, popularized in the U.S. in the 1950's, acted as a filter blocking most people's ability to see who I really was.

Fortunately, this wasn't my first rodeo with preconceived ideas.

After running the nearly 100% male gauntlet that led to my Mechanical Engineering degree, battling preconceived ideas about who I was and what I was capable of was second nature, so I knew what I had to do. With the right attitude, the courage to challenge people's beliefs and a little luck, I was able to land a job and was back earning nearly double my pre-kid salary in less than a year.

This I expected. What came next, I couldn't have imagined.

In the process of challenging the beliefs of others, I eventually come face to face with the damage caused by my own actions and subconscious beliefs.

Ultimately, it wasn't the bucking of tradition that tossed me, it was my lack of self-awareness that did. I could endure battling a foe I could see. Discovering my own actions had led to costly losses, however, broke me. This is when I stopped, dropped what I knew, and began to get curious about what else I was missing.

It turned out I was missing a lot.

Despite thinking that I was very intuitive and open minded, I learned that my perception of how life was supposed to work was blocking me from seeing possibilities and leading me to unintentionally perpetuate and amplify conflict. To neutralize my defenses and open to hidden possibilities, I had to learn to become aware of the beliefs I used to guide my actions, and then leave them behind before I entered the realm of another's beliefs, ideas, and experiences. When I did, breakthroughs in thinking and understanding occurred, leading to bridges across divides, impossible becoming possible, deep hurts healing, and new connections being created.

When it came to overcoming life's obstacles, rising from adversity, and navigating uncertainty, it became clear that 'taking my shoes off first' was a critical part of each journey. Since 2016, I have been sharing this lesson with my clients, helping them break through often invisible barriers so they could achieve better results in all aspects of their lives.

When I discovered my clients were sharing the idea of 'taking your shoes off first' with their spouses and friends, posting it on office walls, and using it in interviews, I knew it was an idea that resonated and needed to be shared more broadly.

The story you are about to read is the best way I could imagine sharing this life changing idea in a memorable way while giving people a glimpse of how easy it is to fall prey to stealthy beliefs.

As a tidal wave of transformational change overwhelms our world demanding that we let go of old ways of thinking and work together globally for the sake of us all, there has never been a more important time for people to open their minds to new possibilities and learn to bridge the divides created by radically different experiences.

Taking your shoes off first is a great place to start.

A Note About the Book

Although what follows is completely fictional, the research and innovations noted within this book are all real. Additionally, each character's story is a representation of real-life transformations – my own or my client's – that came when the concept of 'take your shoes off first' was embraced.

CHAPTER 1

Stop, Drop, and Roll

"Why does it always have to end in battle?" Steve yelled, smacking the steering wheel, and slamming on the brakes. He was so upset by yet another blow-up with his business partner, Mia, that he nearly ran a red light. After 12 years running a successful business together, Steve was mystified as to why they couldn't seem to get through a single strategy session without it turning into a war.

He was convinced Mia was losing her grasp of reality. The biggest piece of evidence was that she had just caused them to lose their biggest client contract — the one that had been paying the bills for almost a decade — and rather than be stressed, she seemed downright relieved about it. It was as if she had no idea where the money that paid for her house and her kids' schools came from.

Rather than asking for forgiveness, she kept pushing to meet with investors to help keep them afloat until they could "digitally transform" the company — whatever that meant to her. Steve couldn't make any sense of Mia's plan because every time she started talking about it, she sounded insane. He was at his limit and had to figure out what to do fast!

Once upon a time, things had been very different. Mia and Steve's view for the company had been in such alignment that it was easy to make the jump from being co-workers at a big company to starting their own. He had been the king of sales and she, the queen of services. Their original service offering was so popular, that within three years they employed over 50 people and now they ran a multi-million-dollar company employing over 100 people.

In the past year, however, their disagreements had become so frequent that tension in the office was palpable. Most of the staff was on edge, wondering when the next blow up would happen.

The problem was that they both knew something needed to change, but they couldn't agree on what.   They both saw things so differently. Lately, it felt as though she were a different person, not someone he had been working with closely for over two decades.

———

It was just after 11p.m. when he walked in the door exhausted, but still amped up. His wife, Ella, came down the stairs and kissed him hello as she walked into the kitchen.

"Hey honey," said Ella. "I finished up my project. It was a beast of a design! I'm so glad to be done."

When Steve didn't respond, Ella went to the

sink and started filling the kettle. "I was going to wind down with some tea. Would you like some?"

Ella knew about the growing discontent with Mia, but she still had hope the two of them could find some way to see eye to eye. She had grown up with Mia and still considered her to be one of her closest friends and business confidants, which was great when all was well. But lately, Ella felt like she was being put in the middle and she was getting tired of it.

Steve shrugged and put his bag down on the dining room table. "Does it come with a shot of whiskey?"

"That bad, huh?" Ella asked, knowing he and Mia had scheduled a 'clear the air' meeting.

"Worse," Steve said, as he went to hang up his jacket and put his keys and wallet on the dresser by the door.

"Let's hear it. What is Mia up to now?" Ella said as she handed Steve a steaming cup of herbal tea.

For the next 20 minutes, Steve let out all his frustration in a blur. He detailed the chaos he believed Mia was causing, but carefully avoided telling Ella about how Mia had cost them their biggest contract. It was one ugly truth she didn't need to hear at this time of night, mainly because Steve didn't want to deal with her reaction to it.

Ella yawned and Steve got the message, so he encouraged her to go to bed.

She nodded and said, "Sorry honey, the girls and I have to get going to the tournament early in the morning." She yawned again before saying, "I know Mia is frustrating you. However, I also know this company means the world to her, so I can't believe that she is trying to sabotage it. I think something else is going on. Is it possible you are missing something?"

This suggestion irritated him. He had bent over backwards trying to make things work for years and it wasn't working, or more likely Mia just wasn't working anymore. He didn't want to fight, so he let it go and just mumbled something

11

about needing to figure it out. Then he kissed Ella goodnight, grabbed his tea and his bag, and headed to the couch.

Ella called after him. "Remember what my Dad always says – When you are hot in the head, you aren't firing on all cylinders, you are on fire and your brain is fried. Stop, Drop and Roll."

Steve just rolled his eyes, sat down, and kicked his feet up onto the coffee table. The lights in the stairwell clicked off and he heard his wife call down. "Did you take your shoes off first?"

He hmphed and thought, 'as if taking my shoes off would help anything.'

However, he knew her father's words might.

Ella's father was a retired Professor of Psychology who now ran a private consultancy and was writing his fourth book. He was known for his research on helping people control their defenses and tap into their critical thinking skills in crisis moments. The military was one of his biggest clients and for good reason. Being able to access critical thinking skills in the middle of an intense conflict was often the difference between life and death in that line of work.

He could hear his father-in law saying, "When your intensity and frustration is rising like a fire burning out of control, Stop, Drop and Roll! You need to put the fire out first because you won't be able to think clearly until you do. When you are on fire you aren't hot, you are fried!"

The steps came back to him:

> *Stop* – first stop what you are doing. Take a breather and calm yourself down.

> *Drop* – drop what you think you know or feel you must do and any other story that is yelling at you.

> *Roll* – get curious and keep being curious until you start to see other possibilities.

His father-in-law's voice was in his head again.

***

"Stop trying to solve the problem and focus instead on trying to understand it. Get curious about what you might be missing."

***

This idea exhausted Steve even further. He didn't want to be curious. He wanted to solve the problem as quickly as possible. That is how he would calm down, he thought.

He couldn't drop anything because Mia already had! She had gone too far this time. "Damnit!" he said audibly, then smacked the couch cushion.

He leaned his head back and closed his eyes, determined to figure out how to handle this mess before he went to bed.

CHAPTER 2

Dreams and Lemmings

Steve hadn't remembered feeling this upset in a long time, maybe not ever. His whole life was on the line and he knew he couldn't speak with Ella about it honestly. Not yet anyway. Since it was still day time in Hawaii, he decided to call his mom to see how she had worked out problems with her co-founder.

Steve's mom had been a successful businesswoman before she married his dad. With an MBA from Stanford, she had been one of those powerhouse women the world needed more of.

But, with the birth of her kids, she found herself stepping away from her executive suite and getting swallowed up by the world of cooking, cleaning, and caring. The mother he knew was 'just a mom' until she rediscovered herself when Steve was in high school. Ultimately, watching her build an international company out of a simple passion for candle making was the reason he had the guts to jump the corporate train and become an entrepreneur himself.

"Hey kiddo, kinda late for you there isn't it?" his mom said as she picked up the phone. Steve shook his head a bit at her habit of calling him 'kiddo' even though he was nearing 40, and then silently admitted he would probably do the same to his own kids.

"Hey Mom," Steve said, stifling a yawn. "Yes, it's late, but I can't sleep. Things with Mia are out of control and I just don't know who to talk to about it. I know you had co-founder hurdles, so I thought you might have some advice."

Steve told his mom he was really worried he

was going to lose everything if he didn't figure out a way to get Mia to stop pushing for a big overhaul of the company and agree to double down on what was working soon.

His mom empathized with how frustrating it can be when you don't see eye to eye with your business partner, and then encouraged him to sleep on it and take some time to figure things out. "You don't want to be a lemming after all!" she said.

"That is what I'm trying to prevent!" exclaimed Steve. "Mia is running off a cliff and I don't want to follow her!"

"That's not what I meant," his mom replied. "My therapist always reminds me that we don't think well when we are stressed. When our mind senses danger, it narrows in on one goal – surviving – and it barrels ahead without thinking. The first lemming off a cliff wasn't following anything but potentially its own fear. The others, however, are failing to think critically and notice what is all around them – including their buddy falling off a cliff to his doom. What I meant is, are you sure you are seeing things clearly or are you just following your fear?"

"Ugh, Mom, I don't have time for your therapist's theories! Just tell me how to get Mia back on course or how I should go about getting her out!"

"I wish I could help, honey, but I don't think you are in the right frame of mind to hear me. You are incredibly gifted in business and you have negotiated your way through some very prickly situations. I'm sure you will figure this one out too. However, I'm concerned that you have forgotten how much you two have gotten through together and how much you are capable of doing."

"What do you mean?" he asked, feeling his angst turn up another notch.

His mom took an audible breath, sighed, and then asked, "Do you remember how much Dad and I used to fight when you were a kid?"

18

"Do I?" he said with biting irony, "I won't be easily forgetting that." He paused to take a deep breath too as memories of what felt like nightly cold wars over dinner followed by screaming matches heard through bedroom doors raced through his head. "I'm amazed at how you guys were able to turn everything around and how you seem so good now."

"It took a lot of work and a great couple's therapist!" his mom admitted. "The first thing our therapist helped us see is that neither of us were feeling good about who we were. We were both depressed, angry, and defensive. Both of us felt as though we had given up all our dreams for the sake of the other. A family had been a dream of ours, but the reality of such responsibility shifted our relationship, and over time we both felt like we were living a life we hadn't asked for. Unfortunately, neither of us could understand what the other was experiencing. We could only see how much we had given up for the other and felt trapped like a couple of caged animals. When you started high school, we were headed for divorce.

"That was about the time I went on that nature retreat to Costa Rica and started becoming obsessed with making natural wax candles."

"Oh, yes, I remember." Steve added, "You took over my bathroom!"

"It was necessary," she said flatly, but with a hint of humor. "Anyway, that retreat was a turning point for me and for our relationship."

"How so?" Steve asked, wondering why he hadn't heard this story before.

"I found a part of me again that I thought I had lost and that I was desperately missing. I found my passion for creation and for driving business. It turns out your dad had been missing that part of me too."

"It was as though a light inside of me had been extinguished by the day-to-day operations of being who I thought I was supposed to be as a mom and a wife. I spent so much time trying to be someone I had to be, but didn't really want to be, that I had grown bitter, but I had no idea.

20

"When I started the company with Joy, we were high on our vision. Everything was new and exciting and hard, and problems abounded, but we felt alive with the challenge of making it all work. I think that positive energy shifted the way your dad saw me.

"Suddenly, he was a resource I could talk to about the business, and he was a great cheerleader. Our interactions became less volatile almost immediately. I saw a part of him I had always admired again and vice versa. Then as the business grew and the stresses of running a business with employees sank in, I started to see the world differently. I became mad at the person I used to be and began to understand why Dad had been frustrated with my flippant remarks about money and his work. I saw how my own mind had been blinding me to how I was acting."

His mom continued, "When I remembered what I was capable of I started to see new possibilities. I had to believe in myself and realize that no matter what happened in my life - conflict, disruptions, or failures – I could always stand back up. That gave me the confidence to wander into the unknown.

"All of this is to say that when I started to live my life in a way that was aligned with who I was, my confidence returned, and my defensiveness retreated. When you feel good about who you are, it's a lot easier to be open to new ideas and see the perspective of another. When you feel threatened or are afraid, anyone who doesn't agree with you feels like an enemy.

"Kiddo, my friends will be here any minute. But before I go, I want you to answer a question for me. Do you really think Mia is trying to sabotage the business or take it from you? Could it be just your perception?"

Steve thought about it for a bit, remembering how much he and Mia had been through. "No," he said, reluctantly. "But I have no idea what she is doing."

"Good," she said with finality. "That is where you want to start."

"Huh? What are you talking about Mom?"

"Not knowing leaves the door open for you to start understanding," she explained. "I was worried that you might be so certain of her guilt that there would be no room for a different outcome."

"Well, I'm sure she messed up!" Steve declared.

"Stop thinking about what she is doing and start thinking about what you are doing. Steve, honey, really ask yourself — are you acting out of strength and confidence? Or out of fear and defensiveness? You want my advice?

***

"Spend time remembering who you are until you feel capable of being curious without being defensive."

***

Steve was just about to protest when he heard

23

voices in the background. His mom squealed in delight at seeing her friends. "Hellooo!" she said in her sing-song voice. She then quickly said she had to go, wished him good luck, and hung up.

Steve was happy that Hawaii retirement life seemed to be suiting her, but he wished she could have explained a bit more before going.

He wasn't sure he had followed everything his mom had said, or how it was related to the situation he was in. It was interesting to know more background on how his parents' marriage had been pulled from the brink of disaster. He took a mental note in case he and Ella ever hit a similar point.

Thinking about all his mom had said, he grudgingly agreed that he and Mia had made it through a lot of tough times. Overall, the past decade had been a lot of fun, especially when they were in the thick of creating something new. But lately it felt like they had reached the end of the line.

Was he afraid? Yes! He was afraid the business

was going to go under and take all their equity with it.

But was that all? Was he missing something?

What had she said was the key? Remembering who she was and how capable she was?

Just then, his phone vibrated with a text. It was from his mom.

"I believe in you, honey. The question is, how much do you believe in you? Enough to let go of what you think you know?"

CHAPTER 3

Contrary to Popular Belief

The next morning, Steve thought he would mull over the situation on a long walk. A few blocks in, he saw his neighbor, Finn, and her dog. They fell into step together and Steve, not wanting to talk about his struggles with Mia, asked, "What cool insight do you have to share with me today?"

Finn was a researcher for a think tank in D.C. and always had some cocktail worthy tidbit to share. Steve loved running into her as what she shared always made him feel smarter later. She didn't disappoint. As they headed toward the local

26

nature trail, she told him about how influential the story you have in your head is for how you experience life – not just your perception of life, but your physical reality.

"In this health study, a researcher asked hotel maids how much exercise they did in a typical week and most of them responded that they didn't exercise at all," Finn explained. "Given that their job was all about physical labor, the researcher found this response odd. Even more so, it seemed odd that the women's bodies weren't more fit given how much daily work they did. So, the researcher wondered if she helped change the story in the hotel maid's minds, would it impact their physical health. After educating a group of maids about how many calories they were burning doing various typical tasks – vacuuming, scrubbing a shower, changing sheets – she discovered that after a month of continuing to do the same work, but thinking about that work with a different story, the hotel maids all emerged healthier. They had lost weight, had lower blood pressure, and become more proportionally fit."

Steve was in awe. "Could the stories people carry in their heads really hold that much sway in how we go about our lives?"

"Isn't it wild?" Finn replied.

***

"The stories you hold are powerful, impacting how you see and engage in the world. Becoming aware of them and their impact helps clear the way for change."

***

Finn felt the eager pull of her dog's leash and said it was time to start her jog. Before she got too far away, she turned back and added, "Unfortunately, most people are unaware of these stories, let alone the power they hold over us."

As he headed for the river path, Steve was still pondering how rewiring the way someone thought could change the way their body responded to an experience.

When the trail turned toward the river, Steve saw his neighbor, Joseph, sitting on a bench. Joseph was a successful manufacturing sales executive that lived a few houses down and had a son the same age as Steve's twin daughters.

Again, wanting to avoid talking about his own troubles, Steve prompted Joseph for updates on his kids.

"Oh, the kids are fine. It's me that is struggling." Joseph said, shaking his head.

Steve knew that Joseph had been laid off two years ago and it had hit him hard. After over a year of looking, Joseph had taken a job that was 'good enough, but not ideal.'

"Care to walk and talk about it?" Steve offered, happy to talk about someone else's struggles and avoid his own. Joseph nodded, stood up to join him, and then shared that he had just been laid off again.

"Oh, man. Sorry to hear it. Was the company struggling?" Steve asked hopefully, thinking it would be an easy story to tell in future interviews.

"It will be!" Joseph scoffed with conviction. "I doubt they will be around by the end of the year. Leadership has no idea what they are doing! I keep getting in trouble for being the one to flag issues and put a halt to production until they are fixed. They hired me for my experience and then they don't listen to me when I tell them what they are doing is wrong? How can they think it is OK to release products that don't work as they should?"

Joseph was visibly flustered. "When your manager is 26 with a wad of investment money in his pocket, I guess they just don't care," he explained with a dismissive flick of his hand.

As they walked, Joseph continued to complain that young people running companies today don't know what they are doing. Steve thought back to what Finn had said and wondered how much this story was impacting how Joseph was showing up in his job. He couldn't imagine this line of thinking was beneficial.

Steve saw the path back towards his house diverge off the main one and, feeling he needed some time to reflect on his own problems, indicated that he was going to head back. He wished Joseph good luck in his interviews, assuring him that he would be an asset to any company. As Steve turned toward the smaller path, however, he wasn't sure he felt that was true anymore. He looked back to wave goodbye to Joseph and noticed what unusual boots he was wearing. They looked really heavy and inflexible. It seemed like a strange choice of shoe for the easy path along the river.

Before disappearing into the tree lined path, Steve saw Finn running back his way, her dog bounding after her happily. Steve waved and then noticed she was running without shoes. He cocked his head in confusion and then wondered how he kept on missing such conspicuous things.

With the peace and quiet of the smaller wooded trail, his mind set to work on the problem of Mia. Thinking of the research on the maids, he wondered what story she had that was getting in her way.

After 15 minutes of walking, he came across a barrier in the path that he simply couldn't get around. Despite being only a half mile from his home, he had to turn back. He swore to no one, cursing the people who maintained the trails, and thought it would have been nice if they had put a sign up where he left Joseph saying the trail was blocked.

Minutes later, he was mortified to see a sign that warned of the trail closure ahead. He then saw two more signs, including one at the turn off point, all of which said the path was closed ahead.

He sighed deeply and spent the rest of the walk wondering what else he had been missing. Was he perhaps like Joseph? Was he blind to how he was showing up and what was happening around him?

Out of curiosity, Steve looked for news online about the company Joseph was working for. He wasn't surprised to see they were going public the following week and were earning a reputation for disrupting the manufacturing industry.

Story indeed, he thought.

CHAPTER 4

Enlightening Discomfort

On his way home, Steve saw the nail salon his wife frequented. She had been trying to get him to go in for a pedicure for years. He could hear her voice saying, "You might like it!" and then his trigger response "Pedicures are for girls. Last time I checked – not a girl!" Ella would then dismiss him saying, "Your loss!"

With stories on his mind, he wondered if this was an example of a limiting story he held. Just then a bottle cap hit him in the cheek. He looked

34

up to see a couple of teens laughing and slapping at each other.

"It's a good thing that didn't hit my eye." Steve said to them sternly, feeling like he was channeling his father. "Pick that up! You're littering."

The girl in the group who apparently had been the one to toss the cap gave him a smirk and a mock apology curtsey as she exclaimed sarcastically, "Sorry Grandpa!" Then she turned her back on him as she laughed and kept walking.

As Steve bent to pick up the cap, he didn't know if he was angrier about the disrespect, or the fact that he had just been called Grandpa. Looking for a garbage can, his eyes noted the nail salon again.

He suddenly felt propelled to prove that he wasn't a grandpa with limiting beliefs but was actually very open minded. Without another thought, he walked into the salon, threw the cap away, and asked for a pedicure.

A petite kind looking woman pointed him to one of the massage chairs. Gratefully it was at the end of the line and not squished between the mom-daughter duo, and the lady that looked strangely like his third-grade teacher. Steve was overwhelmed by the smells and sights of the place and started regretting his decision.

There were two TVs playing different movies with subtitles, and the pop music his daughters listened to was playing overhead. The air smelled of a mix of chemicals and incense, and there must have been 500 different nail polishes displayed on trays, spinning towers, and mini wall shelves, while a hundred tackily decorated fake nails lined a display on the wall. Posters of unnaturally perfect looking feet and hands glowed in the neon light from the flashing "Waxing Here" sign in the window.

The attendant looked at Steve with concern as she pointed to where he should sit. He moved to sit down and put his feet in the water as his eyes fell on the gold, jade, and red fountain with tangerines at the base and the nearby cat sculpture that was perpetually waving one paw. His senses were on overload, and he didn't think he could feel more out of place if he tried. Just then, however, he was shocked to feel the pedicurist blocking his legs. "Take your shoes off first!" she said, laughing.

He shook his head, feeling embarrassed at how distracted he was, and then recommitted to the experience. Steve took his shoes off and put his feet in the warm water.

The feeling of heat felt wonderful and sent a wave of relaxation through his whole body. The attendant pointed to the massage chair controls and helped him get it started. Slowly, the chaos of color and smells receded to the background and all Steve noted was waves of stress releasing from his body. For the first time since that time in college when he tried to walk across fire, he was feeling his feet. Or perhaps, he thought, he was feeling with his feet.

His initial discomfort gave way to curiosity as he became absorbed with what his pedicurist was

37

doing. She moved deftly clipping, soaking, trimming, pushing, scraping, and rubbing his feet in places no one had ever paid attention to, including himself. He had to admit, it felt awesome. When the foot massage part of the experience started, he was convinced. Pedicures were amazing.

He laughed quietly as he realized that he was just like Joseph and the hotel maids. He too had stories that were preventing him from living a better life.

As his pedicure continued, he started to take note of the other women in the salon. They seemed to work as a seamless team. They moved back and forth helping each other get what they needed to do whatever task they were working on. No one was ever idle and although each client had a dedicated pedicurist, none of them seemed to be working in isolation. The chatter amongst them was consistent and cheerful. You could tell this was a community that shared a strong bond.

His pedicurist smiled, pointed to his toes, and asked, "Do you want them rainbow?" Her laugh afterwards let him know she expected him to say no. As she moved to start cleaning up, he made a split minute decision to embrace the new experience fully and said, "Sure! Rainbow toes it is!"

The whole room busted up laughing, and Steve suddenly became aware that he was the focus of a lot of attention. He also felt like he had infiltrated a female community and been surprisingly welcomed. The more he watched the interactions between the clients and the pedicurists, the more he realized these were relationships that were beyond customers, they were loyal patrons, bordering on friends.

He used to drive by salons like this and feel sorry for the people working in them, doing menial labor for so little pay. But now, he found himself envying them for the connection they had with each other. Who was the more successful really? He was envious of the camaraderie in the group and realized how much he had missed having that in his own work. Where had that gone with Mia?

It seemed he was always mad at his partner and the joy that had once flourished in their relationship and the business was gone, replaced by nothing but stress and disappointment. He didn't seem to ever have something nice to say about Mia. All he could see was all the ways she was messing things up. He wondered how that story was impacting his relationship with her, and influencing what he noticed about what she was doing?

He quietly scolded himself,

***

"You need to get curious about the stories you hold and the impact they have on your relationships and what you see."

***

His mind started asking lots of questions. What was his story doing to himself? What even was the story running through his head? Was it like his mom had said, had he lost sight of what was important in his race to be who others thought he should be?

He was afraid, that much he was sure about. But was it just about losing the business? What was it specifically that bothered him about what Mia was proposing? Was he shutting down her ideas like he had shut down the idea that a pedicure could be a nice thing for a guy as well as a girl?

CHAPTER 5

What Shoes Say

Coffee. He needed coffee, and perhaps some nail polish remover.

He still couldn't believe he had rainbow painted toes and if that wasn't bad enough, he needed to wait for them to dry. His choice was wait at the salon or wear some seriously thin flip flops – if you could call them that and carry his shoes. He was starting to get a headache from lack of morning coffee, so he chose the latter.

It was really hard to walk in the flip flops. He

felt ridiculous shuffling across the street. The shoes were so thin, he felt every little bump. They were also super slippery and threatened to shoot off his foot with every step.

When a Great Dane started eyeing his toes in the bright blue spongy material as though it would be a great chew toy, Steve thought he might have made a very big mistake. He shuffled a little faster and bunny hopped into the coffee shop, looking up just in time to see some kids giggling at him.

Now that he could smell the coffee, he stopped caring about what he looked like. He ordered coffee and an egg sandwich and sat down at a nearby table. Although he could tell people were judging his toes, he was surprised to discover that not only did he not care, but he was kind of happy about it. Even more surprising was realizing that he was proud of himself for embracing such an uncomfortable situation and he was feeling more alive than he had in quite some time. He wondered why.

After a few minutes of reverie, someone pulled out the chair across from him suddenly and sat down. He looked up to see his old colleague, George, who had been going through a rough divorce when he last saw him.

"George! Wow! You are exactly the person I need to talk to today. How are you?"

After a brief catch up, Steve told George about what was going on with Mia, believing George would empathize since he had worked with both of them for several years during the rapid growth stage of the company.

"I'm sorry to hear you guys are struggling." George said, nodding his head. "I always admired you two and how aligned you were in what you valued and the vision you had for the company. Despite coming from such different backgrounds, you seemed to have the kind of partnership in which the sum was greater than the parts. You balanced each other out on bad days and amplified each other on good days."

That was not what Steve was hoping or expecting to hear. All the air seemed to leave his sails and he felt adrift in memories of how good things had once been. "Yeah, we were good partners once upon a time."

"Did you know that my ex and I are friendly now?" George asked.

"You are?" Steve asked with surprise, both by the switch in conversation and the idea. George had been in a tumultuous marriage to say the least and the divorce had been even worse. During the years George had worked with Steve and Mia, it was not uncommon for him to be pulled into court to handle various legal claims made by his wildcat wife. They were at each other's throats for years.

"We are." George said calmly.

Steve, struck by the absurdity of this idea, finally took a good long look at his friend, and saw that he did indeed look peaceful. After hearing some of the stories about his Tasmanian Devil like wife, it was really hard to believe that they were able to patch things up.

45

"It took a lot of work, and a lot of putting our egos to the side, but both of us agreed to put the children first and do what was best for them, always. We still have disagreements, but it doesn't blow up anymore."

"How? Please tell me the secret to patching up a relationship after it hits rock-bottom." Steve pleaded, thinking about the argument he had with Mia just the night before. Ugly things had been said and he honestly didn't think it was possible to come back from it.

George glanced at Steve's feet and said, "I recommend keeping your shoes off! With feet like that, why would you ever cover them up?"

Steve gave a fake laugh. "Really, I'm serious. How can you patch up such a monster divide?"

George looked at him intently and said, "I'm serious too. Keep taking your shoes off. It was the key for me to really understand the craziness that was my wife. And here is the wild part. When I was able to do that, her 'crazy' didn't seem so crazy anymore.

"When I finally understood how she was experiencing our exchanges and how she thought about her life, I started to understand how my own actions, as innocent as I thought they were, would have felt terrible to her."

"Seriously?" Steve asked with a grunt of disbelief.

"Yeah, it wasn't easy to get to that point," George said with a tinge of awe in his voice. "But it's a powerful experience when you finally understand how someone else sees the world. It feels like a breakthrough that impacts everything. But to really see it, sometimes it means seeing yourself in a light that is less than flattering.

"To take your proverbial shoes off – meaning your understanding of how the world operates – you have to feel comfortable enough with yourself that you aren't afraid to see yourself from a critical perspective. It's not that you will always see a negative aspect of yourself, but if you want to really understand someone, you have to be open to it."

Steve recalled what his mom had said and mentioned it to George.

"Wise lady, your mom." George said smiling.

"Yes, she is, but don't let her know I said so, OK?" Steve winked and gave a smile.

George chuckled and acted like he was zipping his lips shut.

"Developing confidence in myself that was strong enough to weather insults and negative feedback without flaring defensively was a big hurdle for me." George admitted. "It took quite a long time to master. Actually, it's more of a perpetual project!"

Steve remembered the text his mom had sent him, 'Do you believe in you enough to let go of what you think you know?' He wondered if what George was saying was the same, so he mentioned it.

"Yeah, it sounds like your mom has had a similar experience. Often, what happens when you really understand another, your beliefs are challenged. What you thought was 'right' may actually be wrong. This is what it means to take your shoes off first – you put what you believe is the truth or is 'right' to the side and you become open to seeing someone else's perspective of life as the truth – even if it means it's the exact opposite of what you believe."

"How could the exact opposite of what you believe be right?" Steve challenged, suddenly feeling defensive. "You are a smart, rational person, and you are telling me that you could be 100% wrong?"

"Yes." George said flatly. "Think of it this way. Imagine you have a cylinder." He whipped out a pen and drew a cylinder on a napkin.

"If someone looked at it from the top, what would they see?" he asked.

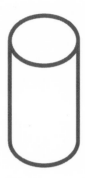

"A circle," Steve said.

"How about from the side at a distance?" George asked.

"A rectangle." Steve was starting to understand.

"Would either perspective be right?"

"Kinda. Well, no, not really." Steve replied, wondering where this was going.

"And yet if you had two people looking at this same object, they would probably argue until the cows came home and perhaps even call each other a few names, in utter disbelief that someone could

50

think a circle is a rectangle and vice versa. In fact, they might even see each other as crazy."

Steve wanted to protest, but George's point was a good one.

"Anyway, when I saw my wife's perspective on our relationship, it became a lot easier to forgive her and a lot easier to engage with her. Seeing the perspective of another, when done in the right way – with your shoes off – is powerful."

***

"It's not enough to walk a mile in someone's shoes.

Whoever came up with that phrase was missing a crucial first step – taking your own shoes off first.

Without taking this step, any effort you make is just your imagination heavily influenced by your own beliefs and experiences."

***

51

Steve sat in silence, contemplating what George was saying.

"Hey, I have to run." George said standing up. "But I'll leave you with one more doozie of a realization. Life got a lot better when I accepted that I couldn't control anyone but myself, including my ex! No matter how hard you try, you can't control what Mia does. You can work to understand and influence her, but all you can do is control how you respond in the face of what she does. And that my friend, can make all the difference." George said, smiling broadly. He gave Steve a pat on his back and wished him good luck before walking away.

For a while Steve just sat there taking in all that had happened that morning. Mostly, however, he wondered about what Mia's truth was. Maybe seeing her perspective would help them repair things to a point in which they could start to build a new understanding. But before he could do that, he would need to learn how to take his own shoes off first.

That was when he noticed his rainbow toes again and his shoes sitting on the bench next to him. He started to notice all the different kinds of shoes on all the people in the coffee shop and began to get curious about the people wearing them and the perspective they brought to even the simplest of things.

He chuckled a little when he heard all the different ways people in line ordered their coffee. Then he imagined what he could tell about each person as a result. Non-fat milk? She was concerned about calories and probably worked out all of the time. Her shoes would be running shoes and she would never let a scone touch her lips. Soymilk latte? He had a sensitive stomach and was likely a vegetarian, so his shoes were probably made of canvas. He would eat a lot of granola and he likely brought his own bags to the farmer's market instead of the grocery store.

Steve noticed his mind was going wild with prescriptions and then he realized he was doing what he always did when he tried to walk a mile in someone's shoes. He was imagining what someone would be like based on beliefs he held. Just as George had said, these were a part of the story he used regularly to make decisions and judge performance – his own and others. His beliefs influenced how he understood everything and ultimately how he behaved. He had to admit, he was barely aware of them.

George was right. Seeing a situation from the perspective of another was harder than he thought. For him to see the perspective of another, he couldn't just imagine it. He had to get curious, ask questions, and be willing to really listen, no matter what he heard, even if it went against what he believed.

This was something he knew he hadn't done much of with Mia in many years. They had been doing the same work for so long, it had become routine and easy. But the past few years, it felt like Mia was always bringing up distractions and trying to mess with a good thing.

Was it possible that some of the underlying beliefs they held weren't as aligned anymore?

CHAPTER 6

Innovate Within

Once his toes were finally dry and his coffee was finished, Steve put his shoes back on and started to walk back home. On the way, he noticed an Open House sign in front of a funky looking modern home. He had never been a fan of modern homes, but he was feeling more open minded this morning and decided to stop in.

At the door, a sign said, "Please take your shoes off first."

It seemed to him that someone was trying to

tell him something. Someone or everyone!

Steve shrugged his shoulders and started taking his shoes off again. Then he remembered his rainbow toes and really wished he had worn socks, and for the second time that day wondered what in the world he was thinking getting his toes painted. Since he didn't see any of the booties he could slip on over his shoes, he decided to keep embracing the discomfort. Although it had been a weird day, it certainly had been an enlightening one, so why stop now he thought.

As soon as he set foot inside the house, he understood why he needed to take his shoes off first. If he hadn't, he wouldn't have understood just how lovely heated wood floors were! Who would have thought heat would make wood floors feel softer?

"Pretty amazing, right?"

The realtor's voice startled him. Until that moment he hadn't realized he had stopped moving and let the stress he was carrying drop away from him as he just enjoyed the radiant heat he was feeling.

"Hmmm...yeah." Steve said in a quieter tone than he had expected. "Really amazing. I can see why you have that sign at the door now and no shoe covers."

"Yeah, it's hard to appreciate the real value of this home if you miss experiencing the little details that make it so special.

"My name is Dee. Feel free to walk through and let me know if you have any questions."

"Is it OK if I just stay here?" Steve asked with a smile.

Dee laughed "Knock your socks off!" and then she gave a thumbs up and a nod towards the rainbow toes and backed away to let Steve explore the house as he pleased. "Be sure to check out the master bath," she added pointing to the stairs with a smile.

Steve moved slowly across the smooth warm

wood floors, checking out the interesting combination of raw building materials and elegant details that flowed throughout the rooms. The whole house seemed to be designed for a different world. There was a specialty outlet in the garage for an electric vehicle that drew power primarily from solar panels set into the windows and on the roof. The trash bin in the kitchen was split into four sections for various recyclables, and there was a compost hole in the kitchen counter that connected directly with an automated compost bin outside.

The entire home was 'smart' enabling you to control virtually every light and device through voice commands, your phone, or touch. Several of the walls moved on tracks in the floor enabling rooms to be opened up, or smaller rooms to be created, and closets were on lockable wheels and could be moved anywhere. It was so different from his traditional idea of what a house should be like, but he could see how it would work really well for a family, adapting to shifting needs as time passed.

"What do you think?" asked Dee as Steve came back into the living room.

Steve was still looking all over as he said, "It's really quite remarkable. I have never seen anything like it before." Then he added, "You were right, the master bath was worth seeing! It's beautiful and I love the idea of a walk-in shower hot tub – if that is what you call it?"

"Whirlpool shower," Dee responded. "And you are right, it's a unique house, right down to how it is being sold."

"What do you mean?" Steve asked with interest. Sales was his area of expertise, so he was always curious to hear about how other people approached it.

Dee invited him to take a seat across from her in the living room. "As you know, when the 2008 crash happened, realtors fell on very hard times. In addition to being underwater on our own investment properties, there was very little work because few people could afford to sell and even fewer could get the loans needed to buy anything.

A lot of us had to take on other jobs if we could find them – bartending for me.

"One night a doctor came in and she was talking about her schedule and how her team of doctors all served the same patients. She said she was resistant to the idea at first and so were the patients as they were used to having one doctor care for them. However, after a few years of struggle, the system of shared care worked better for everyone. Neither patients nor doctors were held hostage by the life events of the other. She said she enjoyed a lot more predictable schedule now and could ramp up or down her hours as she wanted. She also said that she felt like they served their patients better as all their knowledge and skills were pooled together as opposed to just one doctor trying to figure everything out.

"The whole idea got me thinking, could we do the same thing as realtors? No one was excited about their side jobs, and everyone wanted to keep their fingers in the realty world, even if just a little bit."

"You got salespeople to collaborate?" Steve asked with skepticism.

"It took some doing, that is for sure! But, yes, we got REALTORS to collaborate AND put down their territorial defenses." Dee said, nodding her head with eyes wide.

"Their willingness to work together led to streamlining all kinds of tasks and the creation of an app that helps to manage it all. We now share the duties of doing home showing using a credit system – if you show a home you earn credits and then you can ask someone else to show yours, using your credits. The proceeds of sales go into a pot and then it is divided up based on how much everyone worked that month. Just like the doctor had said, we all have much more flexible schedules and can turn up or down our hours based on what is happening in our lives.

"In fact, thanks to automating some processes and playing to our strengths as a team, we can offer much lower fees to our clients, work less, and still get paid about the same hourly rate as we did in our heyday years."

"Dang, that's impressive!" Steve exclaimed with awe and a bit of envy.

"Of course, you can imagine getting to this point required a lot of breakthroughs. There were so many old beliefs and fears we needed to unearth and address. We all had to put our defenses down, and agree that maybe the way we have been doing realty for all this time wasn't the best way – and who wants to admit they have been wrong? Let alone acknowledge that they have been creating their own hell thanks to decades of believing that those who came before had created the perfect system?"

Dee laughed, then shook her head. "There was a lot of trial and error and a lot of people swallowing their pride for the sake of the vision we had for all of us. Just getting it started was so hard! But I have to say, being in crisis mode and realizing something had to change, was a good forcing function to help us all stay committed.

Getting through our fear was the biggest hurdle for sure."

"Wow. I'm glad I decided to stop by," Steve said with a sense of wonder. "You have given me a lot to think about – so much. Thank you for sharing that with me. Would you be open to meeting for coffee sometime so I could learn more about how your system works and how you got to it?"

"Sure, I'd be happy too," Dee said, handing him her card. "I love talking about this! It has certainly been a process, but I have a feeling you might have the right frame of mind to be open to it.

***

"You have to get past what you think is right and integrate the absurd with the rational to discover what else might be possible."

***

Steve put the card in his back pocket and his shoes back on. He took one last look at the house and then continued his walk back home.

He found himself wondering if he was open minded enough to embrace something so radically different from an industry norm like Dee's team had. He thought about how he had been acting in his conversations with Mia and had to admit he wasn't being open minded at all.

A new thought struck him. What if Mia wasn't the problem. What if he was? Was he fighting innovation? Was he blinded by his own stories? Or perhaps his fear?

He took a deep breath and admitted that what was really bothering him was that Mia was proposing to change the business in such a way that what he believed was his superpower – large scale in-person sales – would no longer be critical to the business. Perhaps what he was really reacting to was feeling like he was no longer relevant.

In that moment, Steve was finally aware of the story he had been running, or rather the shoes he had on. He was coming at his conversations with Mia from a place of defensiveness, not growth.

CHAPTER 7

Tall Tales and Fails

As Steve walked through his front door, he saw the picture of his parents on their wedding day hanging on the wall. He wondered if his mom and dad had been in the same head space as he was now when things were at their worst in their marriage. Both his parents would have approached conversations with each other from a place of defensiveness, focusing on how much their lives did not turn out to be what they imagined and doing their best to protect what little they felt like they still had. They were both so afraid, they couldn't let go of what they knew to make room for change and growth.

And now, Steve was doing the same.

He remembered his mom saying that the key to making a positive change in their relationship had been when she believed in herself enough to let go of what was, and opened to what was new in her own life.

He felt like a fool and wondered just how much unnecessary stress and conflict his own fear and blindness to his actions had caused. He could see clearly now how he had blocked productive conversations by failing to be curious and open to new ideas.

Even if he could have a calm conversation with Mia now, however, he doubted it would go anywhere. Things between them had become so heated he didn't know if there was any coming back from it. He started to replay in his head how he knew she would react and all at once his best intentions felt pointless. In fact, she would probably have a hey-day ripping him to shreds as soon as he mentioned that he had been wrong in any way!

In the face of this inevitable future, all his courage and confidence collapsed in on itself and he was once again convinced that he was going to have to cut the cord with her no matter what.

Just then Steve heard a knock on the door.

He opened it to find his neighbor, Jessie smiling back at him. Jessie had been one of his best friends since they moved to the neighborhood five years earlier. At just 35, he had managed to boot strap a digital coaching company that cleared half a million in its second year. He was a bad ass and always good for a few laughs.

Jessie rolled into the house talking a hundred words a minute. He was all amped up because he had just broken a record for his business. He was officially a part of the "Seven Figure Revenue" club he announced proudly and loudly while strutting around the house like a rooster.

After a screeching crow, he exclaimed, "It took

us five years, but we did it! Cocka-doodle-doo! I didn't think we were going to break the code, but we did it!"

Steve shook himself free of his stress enough to be happy for his friend and put his hand up for a big high-five. "What happened? How did you do it?"

Jessie made a beeline for the fridge grabbed two beers and motioned for Steve to join him at the table. "Come my friend, I shall regale you with the tale for a pint of your best ale!" he joked as he twisted off the bottle cap and took a swig.

Steve loved how Jessie treated his home as though it were his own. Jessie felt more like a brother than his own brothers. It had been a few months since they had really hung out, so he knew this 'visit' was headed for three or more beers and he was grateful it was a soccer tournament day. Ella and the girls wouldn't get home until after dinner.

"You know it's been a rough road." Jessie started with a bit of sass.

Steve knew Jessie had jumped headfirst into creating his on-line coaching business and had experienced a lot of early success. However, when one of his clients had written a scathing review of his program, the business took a nosedive. Jessie insisted he had done nothing wrong and tried to fight it, but all his protests only made things worse. With the threat of a lawsuit on their hands and disputes with his co-founder on how to handle it, Jessie and his co-founder went their separate ways. Jessie was left with a broken company and a service offering with terrible reviews. After some reflection and staring into the abyss of returning to corporate life, Jessie made a bold move and publicly owned how he had messed up. Then he started talking honestly about what his failed business experiences had taught him to anyone who would listen. Steve had been in awe of Jessie's ability to be okay with saying how he had messed up and then thrown himself back into rebuilding.

"I know you remember I tried to reboot using a more traditional coaching model, but it just wasn't working. I lost too much money spending time building new programs that nobody wanted. So out of desperation I started selling programs that weren't built just to see if people wanted them. I remember you thought that was a terrible idea and perhaps some of them were. But in the end, it worked! I was able to test ideas a lot faster and that helped me discover what my customers really wanted. The tech that is out there is really opening up doors for us all to become mini-market research people capable of learning what is really important to customers if we are willing to experiment and sometimes look a little foolish in the learning process!

"In the end, my willingness to just throw myself into testing and experimenting, not caring if I got things wrong, but paying attention when my customers responded to what I created helped me find the path to a really killer service."

Jessie raised his eyebrows and took another sip of his beer. Then he smiled and said, "That, my friend, is how I broke the code!

"It wasn't at all how I thought it was going to

71

work out. But it's amazing what happens when you commit to being curious and taking action on your curiosity. It doesn't turn out how you think it will, but that is part of the problem! People keep trying to know the answer before they get to work. To break the code, you don't solve a problem before you act, you solve the problem as you go!"

Steve was struggling to understand and beginning to think about the damage Mia had done using a similar sounding approach. In a slightly tense voice, he asked, "If you don't know the answer you are shooting for, doesn't that lead to a lot of missteps and failures?"

"Steve, don't you see?" Jessie said while slapping him on the back.

***

"Failing is just a part of the journey! It isn't good or bad, it's just a part of learning and iterating!"

***

That's when the dam broke, and Steve's

frustration burst forth. "But Mia lost our biggest account this week and that is REALLY bad!

"She tried to pitch a new concept that I don't think even she understands."

"Well, there is part of the problem! Mia doesn't sell well, and you know that. That is why she needs you!" Jessie exclaimed.

"But she wasn't supposed to be selling anything. The contract was already negotiated by me! She was supposed to be scoping the project and she went totally off the rails...again!" Steve practically yelled. His fury was returning in full force and he knew he was reaching that fried state again. He backed away from the table and took a lap around the house.

When he came back, Jessie said with a sigh, "Wow. I can see why you are frustrated." Then he just sat in silence for a while drinking his beer.

Steve could see he was thinking about something, so he came back to sit at the table and nodded his head towards Jessie, "Give it to me. What are you thinking?"

Jessie took a deep breath and leaned forward towards Steve, "You seem really angry about this. Can you tell me what is behind it?"

Steve looked at him in confusion. Jessie put his hands together in prayer formation and gave him a little namaste bow as if to say please hear me out. Steve sighed, and said, "What do you mean?"

Jessie smiled gently and then explained, "I have learned through my ups and downs in business, and through my yoga practice – that when I get really upset about something, my anger is usually trying to cover up something else I don't want to see or address."

Steve sighed again. Jessie smiled and encouraged him to keep breathing deeply.

After a few moments of reflection, Steve admitted what he had been thinking about prior to getting home. He told Jessie he was afraid that in Mia's new vision for the company, he had no value to add.

"I haven't really engaged in our conversations about the future other than to insist that we double down on what we are good at. I have been spending so much time thinking about how she is messing up, confusing both me and our clients so much that everything is in chaos, that it didn't occur to me that maybe I was the one messing up."

That's when it hit him.

Perhaps what Mia had been asking for all along was that she wanted him to help her with structuring a new service. A part of what made him so good at sales was his ability to structure a package that spoke exactly to the customer's needs and fears. Yes, the need for him to go out and sell directly would be going away in her new model for the business, but his ability to think like the customer and architect sales packages would be something they would need more of as they scaled.

"Damn. It's not all Mia's fault," Steve said, with

a little bit of sadness and relief all at the same time.

"Sounds like you've had a bit of a breakthrough," Jessie said, smiling. "Keep opening up to that line of thinking, my friend. And remember, being wrong is a part of the journey."

Jessie continued, "Hey, I gotta run. I'm taking the wifey to a nice dinner to celebrate."

He finished his last drop of beer and walked to the door, "You got this, Steve. You and Mia are too good a team for it to fall apart over this."

CHAPTER 8

Put a Stake in It

A few hours later, Ella and the girls came home from their long day of soccer games. Both of his girls had really taken to the sport and were lucky enough to have made it onto the same team. Being twins, life was always easier when they could be together.

"Dad! We finally pulled off the taco twist!" his daughters screamed in unison, bounding up to give him a hug.

"Oh wow!" Steve said trying to match their

77

enthusiasm. "Please tell me what the taco twist is."

"It's an offensive strategy the girls have been working on with their team all season," Ella explained. "The girls love it because they named it."

"You tell him mom – we need showers!" he heard as the girls disappeared up the stairs.

Ella laughed as she put her stuff down on the counter. "The girls are very excited both about their performance and how this complicated maneuver helped them score the winning goal in the finals."

After putting her coat and shoes away, Ella grabbed some water and took a seat next to him at the table. "The move is really risky, kind of an all or nothing thing. Once the girls set it up, they must commit, or the other team could easily intercept the ball. The girls have been afraid to try it, but their coach told them it was the only way they were going to get around the other team's defenses. So, the girls put their stake in the ground so to speak and went for it. I was really proud of them for holding their own against such a fierce team. We all were." Ella finished with a contented look. "How was your day?"

"Interesting," Steve said, pointing at his toes.

Ella looked down to see his brightly colored rainbow toes and gave a little giggle. "I can see you finally took my advice. Did you enjoy it?"

"I definitely did. I also think I figured out how I'm going to handle the situation with Mia."

Ella looked at him nervously, "Oh, good. Do I want to know?"

"It's OK. It's going to be hard, but I think I'm ready to hear things from her side. I really haven't been open to hearing her because I have been too worried about the business. I'm still extremely worried about the business – she lost our biggest client last week." Steve finally told her.

"She what?" Ella asked with alarm. "Why didn't you tell me that last night?"

79

Steve just looked at her with a look of expectation, knowing she would eventually understand.

"OK, no, I was not in the right headspace to hear that news." Ella admitted.

Steve smiled, "And that has been my problem. I haven't been in the right headspace to hear what Mia has been trying to tell me. I can see that now. I'll tell you more later, but for right now, I need to plan for a taco twist." Steve winked, trying to look more confident than he felt.

"Whatever you say, honey," laughed Ella. "I'm glad to hear you feel like you see a new path forward."

She smiled and added extra encouragement,

***

"Apply all you have learned and commit to making it work!"

***

Nodding, Steve said, "Mia and I still have to work through some things to get there, but I'm ready to commit to trying some new approaches. I just need to be intentional about how I engage her. Just like the team the girls faced, she is a fierce foe."

"She is an even better friend." Ella reminded him.

"True. And a partner that deserves the best of me, just like you do," Steve said, feeling the truth in this claim more deeply than he had expected. He gave her a kiss and headed back to the living room to work on a plan. Just as he was about to leave the kitchen, he looked back and said, "Hey – you were right. I did need to take my shoes off first."

———

Steve sat down to reflect on all he had learned that day. He knew that if he could share what he had learned, he and Mia were going to have a much better chance of patching up the rift that currently divided them.

He looked down at his rainbow toes and thought about how the experience of doing something so far out of his comfort zone had shocked his whole system into experiencing and engaging in life in new ways. He remembered the nail salon and noted that when everything was unfamiliar, he noticed so much more. This new awareness caused him to question long held beliefs, of which he was barely aware, that had shaped his decisions and experiences for most of his life.

Both his belief that pedicures were only for girls, and his belief that what you did mattered far more than who you did it with or how you did it, had been challenged and proven irrelevant or rather completely false!

Being willing to let go of what he believed he knew was the first step. He grabbed his notepad and wrote:

'Take your shoes off first –

to really open to unknown possibilities, it's important to recognize the beliefs you hold and develop a habit of questioning their relevance and how they shape what you see, feel, and understand. It's only when you are able to set your beliefs to the side that you can see beyond your understanding.'

He wanted to understand more about what Mia was seeing. To do that, he knew he had to put some 'stakes in the ground' and intentionally close the door on blaming Mia. Steve wanted to own his part of the broken bridge between them, even if Mia wouldn't reciprocate. He hoped he could make room to really hear her.

Steve got out his computer and started composing an email to Mia. In it, hoping to set a conciliatory tone, he admitted how he had failed to be the partner he believed it was important to be. Then he invited her to join him to get sushi. It had been many years since they had gone, but he had a feeling that going to the place where they

83

had originally brainstormed the idea for the business would be the right setting for a better meeting.

It was an unusual restaurant that created space for real authentic communication. Before you could be seated, you had to take your shoes off first.

Afterword

What did you take from this story? What meaning did you make?

It's only one short story but people walk away with so many different meanings. Although there is definitely a theme to everyone's interpretation – the specifics and extra meaning varies dramatically. That is the beauty of the story you just read. It resonates on many levels in many different ways.

Since the key point to the story is to help people understand how easy it is to be fooled by their own beliefs, it seems fitting that people read the story and walk away with different ideas. In fact, if you re-read the book later, it's very possible that you would see something different depending on what was happening in your life. There is a ton jammed in here!

What you see and understand is heavily influenced by your beliefs and experiences.

Why is this so important to keep in mind?

If you and I see something different in a situation, how well do you think our conversation will go? If you are trying to get me to open up to a new idea, but the idea feels threatening to me because of how I view the world, how likely is it that I will be open to hearing you? When I react defensively or with anger to something you say which you feel is benign or even kind, how will I appear to you? What is your action likely to be? How will I feel in response?

Your mind is a tricky beast that works quickly to assign meaning to whatever information comes in, categorizing it based on your prior knowledge. This is done at both conscious and subconscious levels in an effort to protect you. Unfortunately, this quick categorization of ideas, often leads people to misinterpret a situation or shut down possibilities before they are understood.

The way to clear the path for new ideas and possibilities – whether for yourself, your relationships, or your career – is to learn to become aware of the beliefs you hold and how they impact your meaning making capacity. Then, learn to put your influential meaning making filter to the side so you can really be open to change. This is what it means to take your shoes off first.

Taking your shoes off first is a simple idea that is easier said than done. To do it well takes practice and an investment in developing yourself. However, when you put in the conscious effort, taking your shoes off first can create the conditions needed for you to achieve breakthroughs in thinking by helping you see new paths and possibilities that were previously hidden to you. The result can be nothing short of miraculous, as strife is neutralized, connections are enriched, and you become more innovative, more collaborative, more inclusive, and more content in life.

Why is it important to develop yourself?

As illustrated in the story, it takes a calm and centered mind to consider new ideas.

When your defenses trigger, your human nature narrows in on threats, gets you ready to fight or flee, but sabotages your ability to critically think and be open to new ideas in the process. When you are trying to overcome a big challenge or a messy problem, this is not helpful.

When you spend time building up your sense of self-worth and confidence in your abilities, you have the reserves and the mindset needed to be reflective and open.

How does this story help?

Beneath this story lies a powerful framework called the Breakthrough Compass which is based on human nature. This framework follows the natural path humans use to reach wiser more intellectually and emotionally evolved versions of themselves. By learning to take your shoes off first, you are helping yourself tap into your natural change capabilities so you can get human nature to work for you rather than against you.

If you noted the ideas highlighted in each chapter of the story, you would get a sense of this framework. Steve was guided through the framework by each of the characters in the book. Each played a key role in helping him see more and evolve his thinking. The framework can be found on my website but for now you can experience it by following the steps Steve took to take his shoes off first.

An overview of Steve's journey and instructions on *how* to take your shoes off first can be found in the following pages to help you:

1. Get the most out of the lessons in this book.

2. Help you remember key points when you want to refer to them quickly.

3. Inspire curiosity in you about how impactful it could be for you or your team to learn how to harness a natural strength of all humans – the ability to evolve – to let go of what has been to become what can be.

How do you learn more?

There are many resources available on-line, including a template detailing an exercise to help you master the art of becoming aware of your beliefs and then make room for new ones. It is called the Rule of ALSO.

Additionally, if you want to learn more about how to develop the skills needed to execute on the lessons presented in this book or bring this idea to your community or organization, please check out the resources, and learn about coaching, workshops, assessments, and online programs at

TakeYourShoesOffFirst.com.

A Final Note

If you choose to pass this book on to someone you believe it will inspire, **thank you!**

Through sharing this book and the idea of taking your shoes off first you are helping to bring more light and shared understanding to lives everywhere.

If you want to help more people embrace this idea, please consider leaving a review on **Amazon.com** so more people will see this book!

I hope you believe as I do, that the world can become a better place for us all if more people know how to *take their shoes off first*.

.

Take Your Shoes Off First (Your Pocket Guide)

Although there are eight key lessons I want to highlight, this story is filled with much more. I love speaking with people after they have read the book because they often surprise me with a new lesson or application for the story. Which brings me to a primary idea of the book:

There are many truths and infinite possibilities.

What you see and understand is heavily influenced by your beliefs and experiences.

Whenever I am up against a problem or a challenge that feels overwhelming, I try to remember this idea and immediately I feel a little better. Then I work to take my shoes off first before doing anything else, knowing that if I do, I will be making room for change to help me out of my predicament.

93

The following lessons will help you take your shoes off first. They reflect your natural process to become a wiser version of yourself. When you follow these steps, you can get to better easier and faster.

Summary of Lessons:

1. Believe in infinite possibilities and get curious.
2. Believe in you, the real you.
3. Open to your faults.
4. Be open to what lies beyond the surface.
5. Put your beliefs to the side and listen for others.
6. Disrupt status quo.
7. Accept that failing is a part of the journey.
8. Intentionally cross the threshold and close the door behind you.

(Each are expanded upon in the following pages.)

In Chapter 1, Steve is reminded by his wife to let go of what he believes is right and get curious about what he might be missing. She refers to her Dad's mantra – "Stop, Drop and Roll" – a mnemonic to remember in high stress times when you find yourself fighting fires haphazardly, to:

1. *Stop* what you are doing.
2. *Drop* what you believe you must do.
3. *Roll* with curiosity, believe in infinite possibilities, and make room for change.

Lesson 1:

Believe in infinite possibilities and get curious.

Stop trying to solve the problem. Let go of what you think you know and start asking questions.

In Chapter 2, Steve learns from his mom about how easy it is to be fooled by his emotions into sabotaging his own interests and future. She tells him that her marriage almost ended in divorce because every interaction was poisoned by her negative state of mind. When she revived her sense of confidence and belief in herself, her defensiveness subsided, and their connection returned. She encouraged him to consider if he was acting out of strength and confidence, or out of fear and defensiveness.

Lesson 2:

Believe in you, the real you.

Have faith in your ability to handle what comes. When you are calm and at peace with self, you think better and can respond rather than react since you are able access the critical thinking portion of your brain.

In the beginning of Chapter 3, Steve learns from his neighbors, Finn and Joseph, about the power of the stories we tell ourselves and how they direct our brain often without our knowing. After Steve gets curious about how others are impacted by the stories they tell, he begins to notice how his own brain causes him to miss basic things in his life.

Lesson 3:

Open to your faults.

You can't find the solution until you accept you are a part of the problem. You have a role to play even if that role is just how your own brain is limiting what you are capable of seeing.

In Chapter 4, Steve chooses to test the impact of his beliefs, dives into unfamiliar territory, and discovers just how limiting his beliefs can be. When he engages in the new experience of a pedicure, his awareness is heightened and he discovers that while disorienting, it is also enlightening to be so present with his surroundings. He begins to wonder what else he has been artificially blinding himself to.

Lesson 4:

Be open to what lies beyond the surface.

You hold a set of beliefs that you are often unaware of and they influence your actions, your decisions, and the outcome of all interactions. Without knowing what these beliefs are, you can't make sure they aren't blocking you from seeing what you are missing.

In Chapter 5, Steve learns about the power of perspective. After listening to how his friend, George, was able to turn a bitter divorce into a collaborative parenting relationship, Steve begins to see the power of taking your shoes off first. If you don't, any effort to understand the perspective of another is just your imagination heavily influenced by your beliefs and experiences.

Lesson 5:

Put your beliefs to the side and listen for others.

To expand your understanding, work to understand the world from a different perspective. To do that, take your shoes off first, meaning put your beliefs and perspectives to the side, and then walk in another's, seeking to really see the world as they see it, not as you see it.

In Chapter 6, Steve realizes how hard it can be to let go of what you know and believe to be right. While speaking with Dee, the realtor, Steve acknowledges the amount of fear that needs to be overcome and wild ideas that need to be considered before a new approach can be embraced. It is in this chapter that he finally realizes that he has been closed to hearing other ideas.

Lesson 6:

Disrupt status quo.

New possibilities can only be realized when you work to overcome your fear and apply new perspectives to old problems and are willing to replace old traditions with new approaches.

———

In Chapter 7, Steve comes face to face with one of his most damaging and limiting beliefs – the idea that failing is not an option. His best friend Jessie helps him begin to see how he has been fighting against a demon that didn't exist. He realizes that if he had only been more curious and less defensive, he would have been able to see it and avoid a lot of the battles with Mia.

Lesson 7:

Accept that failing is a part of the journey.

All the thinking in the world isn't going to lead to better results if action isn't taken. Solve the problem as you go, accepting that getting it wrong is a part of the journey.

In Chapter 8, Steve learns that to truly integrate new learning, you must commit. He acknowledges to himself and Ella that he hasn't been in the right headspace to listen to Mia. Inspired by his daughters' actions on the field, Steve commits to being intentional with his actions to integrate all he has learned to create a new outcome for his interactions with Mia.

Lesson 8:

Intentionally cross the threshold and close the door behind you.

Breakthrough is realized when you commit to integrating new insights into intentional actions aimed at closing the door to old and walking bravely into new.

———

Notes

(What other lessons did you note?)

Individual Reflection Guide

1. What parts of the story resonated the most for you and why?

2. What bothered you in the story and why?

3. The research about the maids is real and has been backed up by similar research studies showing the physical and chemical impact of our perceptions and beliefs. What beliefs do you hold that might be creating a physical benefit or drag in your life? (e.g. I believe I need 8 hours of sleep. How does that belief impact you? Consider beliefs about your career, relationships, family, love, future, etc.)

4. What stories are you running in your head about a challenge you are facing? How might these stories be limiting your ability to solve the challenge?

5. What you see and understand is heavily influenced by your beliefs and experiences. Think of a current difficult situation or relationship. Do you think other people see what you see? Why or why not? What beliefs influence what you see?

*Be sure to go to **TakeYourShoesOffFirst.com** for additional resources and exercises to help you make the most of the lessons in this book.***

Group Discussion Guide

In a group, discuss the following:

(Consider having people write their answers down and then share them with the group so answers aren't influenced by hearing another's.)

1. In your own words, what is this book about?

2. What resonated for you in the book? What bothered you about it?

3. How do you think your experiences and beliefs influence how you interpreted the book?

4. What practice from the book would you like to see your group adopt? Why?

5. What are the stories or beliefs of your organization and culture that influence how decisions are made and actions are taken? Are these stories helpful or hurtful to progress towards goals?

Resources

TakeYourShoesOffFirst.com

Rule of ALSO:

This tool will run you through an eye-opening exercise designed to help you open your mind to ideas and perspectives that are currently hidden to you.

For Teams / Organizations:

Asking your team or organization to read "Take Your Shoes Off First" before strategy sessions or the launch of big change initiatives can help set the tone for breakthrough conversations to happen. It is also easily integrated into new manager training, diversity and inclusion efforts, and leadership coaching programs.

111

Workshop curriculum and facilitation ideas are available centered around these themes:

- Increasing Adaptability

- Building Healthy Relationships

- Minimizing conflict and maximizing collaboration

- Accelerating Innovation

- Inclusion and Belonging

Other Resources:
- Status Quo Defender Assessment
- Breakthrough Coaching
- Breakthrough Compass
- Workshops, Facilitation, Group Coaching
- Books
- Blogs
- Videos

Acknowledgements

This book exists because of these people, and I am grateful.

My first clients who put their trust in me to help them get through the hurdles before them, and then encouraged me repeatedly to share my ideas with more than just moms.

Scott Santucci who believed in me until I could believe in myself. He helped me see how blind I was about many things, including the value of my "little shoe idea."

Anne Weber – my editor, my friend, and my client who just took a little longer to "bloom." She always adds a little extra spirit to the experience.

TK Palad – for the cover art. Few words, amazing illustration.

AND

I am so grateful for
my <u>amazing family</u> who has supported me
through it all!

Especially these rascals who have kept me sane,
laughing, driven, and hopeful:

Zack, Amelia, and Cormac

About the Author

Julia Freeland is a coach and professional development strategist focused on helping people thrive in change. In 2016, she found herself getting fired from her dream job only six months after receiving the highest accolades of her career. She spent the next four years and $250K to discover why and develop a strategy to help others avoid the same fate and improve their ability to navigate disruption and transitions. Her life-long passion for understanding and developing people is only rivaled by her love of beach volleyball and spending time with her three precocious kids.

This is her first published book. More are coming...

Learn more at **revolveyou.com** or
TakeYourShoesOffFirst.com

Take Your Shoes Off First

Made in the USA
Middletown, DE
15 September 2021